# The Elephants in the Room!
## A. Ernest Endeavor

All rights reserved. No part of this book may be reproduced in any form or by any means without prior consent of the Publisher, except brief quotes used in reviews.

ISBN 978-1-935825-15-9

Printed in the United States of America

10 9 8 7 6 5 4 3 2 1

©copyright A. Ernest Endeavors 2018

A Ernest Endeavor

"These are the times that try men's souls; the summer soldier and the sunshine patriot will, in this crisis, shrink from the service of his country; but he that stands it now, deserves the love and thanks of man and woman. Tyranny, like hell, is not easily conquered; yet we have this consolation with us, that the harder the conflict, the more glorious the triumph."

Thomas Paine<br>The American Crisis

*The Elephants In The Room!*

"History is the poisoned well, seeping into the ground-water. It's not the unknown past we're doomed to repeat, but the past we know. Every recorded event is a brick of potential, of precedent, thrown into the future. Eventually, the idea will hit someone in the back of the head. This is the duplicity of history: an idea recorded will become an idea resurrected. Out of the fertile ground, the compost of history."

Anne Michaels
Fugitive Pieces

A Ernest Endeavor

## Table of Contents

Chapter 1 Psychological Slavery ................................................. 5

Chapter 2 Institutionalized ......................................................... 10

Chapter 3 The Stranger .............................................................. 14

Chapter 4 The Wives of Abraham .............................................. 20

Chapter 5 Four Very Special Women ......................................... 26

Chapter 6 A Kingdom Divided ................................................... 32

Chapter 7 Excuses ....................................................................... 36

Chapter 8 An Unholy Harvest .................................................... 41

Chapter 9 Lost In Translation .................................................... 46

Chapter 10 Major Engagements ................................................. 52

Chapter 11 The Golden Rule ...................................................... 56

Chapter 12 Surgical Coma .......................................................... 63

Chapter 13 Hypocrisy ................................................................. 67

Chapter 14 The Plot Thickens .................................................... 72

Chapter 1 God Is Unfair Book 2 Preview ................................. 81

Chapter 2 The Original Pimp Part 1 Book 2 Preview ............. 90

Chapter 3 Military Etiquette Book 2 Preview ......................... 95

# Chapter 1
# Psychological Slavery

I've often heard people say, "an elephant never forgets." Zoologists say that's because the elephant can only memorize a few things which explains why the fully-grown animal that weighs up to 7-tons, can be held captive by a short rope tied to a stake in the ground. Even though he's much larger and weighs tons more than he did at his birth (200 lbs.), his memory enslaves him to the past. If he could talk, he'd probably say, "This is it for me. This is all there is. I'll never be free because this stake I'm tied to won't let me go." The elephant doesn't know that the only thing constraining him is his mind.

This concept is equally true of the children of Israel, who God, through Moses, freed after 430 years of captivity. Spiritually speaking, Israel never really left Egypt because their minds were still in Egypt even though their bodies were approaching the promised land. God first established a covenant with Abraham while his name was still Abram, before Isaac was conceived, with the foreknowledge that his descendants would suffer 400 years of captivity. Genesis 15:13 "Then He said to Abram: "Know certainly that your descendants will be strangers in a land *that is* not theirs, and will serve them, and they will afflict them four hundred years. [14] And also the nation whom they serve I will judge; afterward they shall come out with great possessions." Genesis 15:18 "On the same day the Lord made a covenant with Abram, saying: "To your descendants I have given this land, from the river of Egypt to the great river, the River Euphrates— [19] the Kenites, the Kenezzites, the Kadmonites, [20] the Hittites, the Perizzites, the Rephaim, [21] the Amorites, the Canaanites, the Girgashites, and the Jebusites."

    Nearly four-hundred and thirty years had passed, and God was ready to make good on his promise to Abraham. Through the wonder of a burning bush, that was not consumed by the fire, He spoke to Moses, who he knew was a fugitive at large for murdering an Egyptian. The punishment for such a crime was death. Genesis 9:5 "Surely for your lifeblood I will demand *a reckoning;* from the hand of every beast I will require it, and from the hand of man. From the hand of every man's brother I will require the life of man. 6 "Whoever sheds man's blood, By man his blood shall be shed; For in the image of God He made man."

It must be noted that the call came while Moses was in a state of sin. There was no offer of salvation and no confession of sin by way of the sinner's prayer. Yet Moses had clearly broken the law, but God made him the lawgiver by extending remarkable grace, giving him The Ten Commandments, which included a directive against murder. This was a prelude to what Jesus explained in Matthew 12:31 and the mercy shown to Cain in Genesis 4.

God did not choose an army of men. He chose one man to speak on his behave, but He himself was the army that would overthrow Egypt. Exodus 3:8 "So I have come down to deliver them out of the hand of the Egyptians, and to bring them up from that land to a good and large land, to a land flowing with milk and honey, to the place of the Canaanites and the Hittites and the Amorites and the Perizzites and the Hivites and the Jebusites. Later, He reminds the children of Israel of the covenant he made with Abraham. Leviticus 20:24 But I have said to you, "You shall inherit their land,

and I will give it to you to possess, a land flowing with milk and honey." I *am* the Lord your God, who has separated you from the peoples.

In other words, the children of Israel were going to the land of plenty, but twenty-one and a half generations of slavery, under hard taskmasters, made it impossible to break away from the psychological servitude they were accustomed to. Proverbs 23:7a "For as he thinks in his heart, so is he."

Even though they were free, they still thought like slaves. They still talked like slaves. They still acted like slaves, and eventually they became slaves again. Exodus 16:2 "Then the whole congregation of the children of Israel complained against Moses and Aaron in the wilderness. 3 And the children of Israel said to them, 'Oh, that we had died by the hand of the Lord in the land of Egypt, when we sat by the pots of meat *and* when we ate bread to the full! For you have brought us out into this wilderness to kill this whole assembly with hunger.'"

A couple verses later, Moses responds to their complaints with the following: Exodus 16:8 "*This shall be seen* when the Lord gives you meat to eat in the evening, and in the morning bread to the full; for the Lord hears your complaints which you make against Him. And what *are* we? Your complaints *are* not against us but against the Lord."

The problem was their thinking. Their minds were so inured to the brutally of Egyptian slavery, that freedom from it had very little value and they were all too willing to return to it. Romans 12:2 "And do not be conformed to this world, but be transformed by the renewing of your mind, that you may prove what *is* that good and acceptable and perfect will of God."

But what of today's church?

A Ernest Endeavor

## Chapter 2
## Institutionalized

Is the 21st century church any different than their spiritual forefathers, who after leaving a demoralized Egypt, willfully shackled themselves to that which was most familiar? Freedom was uncomfortable. They didn't know what was going to happen from day to day. In Egypt, under the rule of a Pharaoh, they had a schedule and a daily quota of bricks to fulfill. But with the God who freed them, there seemed to be a lot of uncertainty. In their minds, that made their emancipator unreliable. They didn't know what they were going to eat or when. And water? Where was it?

Think of it. Whole families thought they were going to starve to death or die of thirst. Wives were probably looking to their husbands for answers to this puzzling dilemma—freedom and an agonizing death. Or life and the certainties of slavery? It was an easy choice for them. Husbands, having no answers, yet being constantly pressured by the voice of their wives (Genesis 3:17) and the unrelenting sound of their children crying day and night probably drove them to demand answers from Moses and Aaron, men they could see, rather than a God they could not see. How quickly they had forgotten the majesty of God and the methodical overthrow of those who had been their masters for 430 years? It never even occurred to them to ask God for the sustenance they needed (James 4:2d).

They were institutionalized.

Has the slave mind been bequeathed to 21$^{st}$ century Christians? If so, that contradicts John 8:36 "Therefore if the Son makes you free, you shall be free indeed." Is the 21$^{st}$ century church free indeed? Or having been freed as Christ said, has the church chosen to reject the scriptures that set them free to embrace that which enslaves them? That begs the question: If a Christian rejects the scriptures, is he a Christian?

Galatians 3:28 says, 'There is neither Jew nor Greek, there is neither slave nor free, there is neither male nor female; for you are all one in Christ Jesus.' On the surface, this verse seems contradictory. Clearly, there are Jews and Greeks. There are men and women. And slavery is still being practiced on the earth. What is this verse about? It's about the family of The Most High God! The family of God is not filled with Jews only, but all nations—those who have accepted Christ is the only savior. I Timothy 2:5 "For *there is* one God and one Mediator between God and men, *the* Man Christ Jesus."

It's a family that has been separated from flesh and blood—DNA. It is a spiritual family, and it is expected to be function as those who have been chosen, handpicked by God himself. Ephesians 1:4 "just as He chose us in Him before the foundation of the world, that we should be holy and without blame before Him in love, ⁵having predestined us to adoption as sons by Jesus Christ to Himself, according to the good pleasure of His will, ⁶to the praise of the glory of His grace, by which He made us accepted in the Beloved."

John 10:16 "And other sheep I have which are not of this fold; them also I must bring, and they will hear My voice; and there will be one flock and one shepherd." If there's any confusion as to who the "one flock" are, Mark 16:15 makes it clear, And He (Jesus)

*The Elephants In The Room!*

said to them, "Go into all the world and preach the gospel to every creature."

According to Exodus 12:38 A mixed multitude went up with them also, and flocks and herds—a great deal of livestock. I think it's safe to say that the mixed multitude were not of the household of Israel. The mixed multitude were the "strangers" among them. We can conclude, therefore, that whoever accepts Christ as both Lord & Savior is in the family of God, right?

The problem was their thinking, which is why God tells his people renew their minds. Romans 12:2 "And do not be conformed to this world, but be transformed by the renewing of your mind, that you may prove what *is* that good and acceptable and perfect will of God."

A Ernest Endeavor

# Chapter 3
# The Stranger

Why is the family of God still adhering to Jim Crow mentality, reminiscent of the elephant and the Hebrew slave? Neither of whom could fully embrace freedom because their minds were and are anchored to the past. Paul, in his letters taught that the fetters of race have been eradicated through Christ. Galatians 3:28 "And the Scripture, foreseeing that God would justify the Gentiles by faith, preached the gospel to Abraham beforehand, *saying,* 'In you all the nations shall be blessed.'" Colossians 3:11 where there is neither Greek nor Jew, circumcised nor uncircumcised, barbarian, Scythian, slave *nor* free, but Christ *is* all and in all.

By the way, this race business is not a contemporary concept, but rather a runniness construct, thousands of years in the making, designed to weaken, disable, and imprison the mind permanently, making the slavery of sin not only acceptable, but making it a shrouded desire. This school of thought is the true strength of "street knowledge", better known as "keeping it *real*".

The bible, however, extensively teaches that a "stranger" was always accepted if he converted to the Hebrew faith, which meant he had to accept the Hebrew God on His terms. Consider, for example, Exodus 12:48 "And when a stranger dwells with you *and wants* to keep the Passover to the Lord, let all his males be circumcised, and then let him come near and keep it; and he shall be as a native of the land. For no uncircumcised person shall eat it. [49] One law shall be for the native-born and for the stranger who dwells among you."

The stranger engaged in the Sabbath: Exodus 20:10 "but the seventh day *is* the Sabbath of the Lord your God. *In it* you shall do no work: you, nor your son, nor your daughter, nor your male servant, nor your female servant, nor your cattle, nor your stranger who *is* within your gates."

The stranger was not to be mistreated, but rather loved as much as one loved himself: Leviticus 19:33 "And if a stranger dwells with you in your land, you shall not mistreat him. [34] The stranger who dwells among you shall be to you as one born among you, and you shall love him as yourself; for you were strangers in the land of Egypt: I *am* the Lord your God."

The stranger suffered the same punishment: Leviticus 20:2 "Again, you shall say to the children of Israel: 'Whoever of the children of Israel, or of the strangers who dwell in Israel, who gives *any* of his descendants to Molech, he shall surely be put to death. The people of the land shall stone him with stones."

The stranger's benefits were unending: Numbers 15:15 "One ordinance *shall be* for you of the assembly and for the stranger who dwells *with you,* an ordinance forever throughout your generations; as you are, so shall the stranger be before the Lord. [16] One law and one custom shall be for you and for the stranger who dwells with you."

The stranger was not to be treated differently in court: Deuteronomy 1:16 "Then I commanded your judges at that time, saying, 'Hear *the cases* between your brethren, and judge righteously between a man and his brother or the stranger who is with him."

Every third year the stranger was afforded the same right to eat as the priests, the widows, and the fatherless: Deuteronomy 14:28

"At the end of *every* third year you shall bring out the tithe of your produce of that year and store *it* up within your gates. ²⁹And the Levite, because he has no portion nor inheritance with you, and the stranger and the fatherless and the widow who *are* within your gates, may come and eat and be satisfied, that the Lord your God may bless you in all the work of your hand which you do."

The stranger was allowed to worship before the lord: Deuteronomy 16:11 "You shall rejoice before the Lord your God, you and your son and your daughter, your male servant and your female servant, the Levite who *is* within your gates, the stranger and the fatherless and the widow who *are* among you, at the place where the Lord your God chooses to make His name abide. ¹²And you shall remember that you were a slave in Egypt, and you shall be careful to observe these statutes."

The stranger was given part of the tithe along with the Priests, the widow, and the fatherless: Deuteronomy 26:12 "When you have finished laying aside all the tithe of your increase in the third year—the year of tithing—and have given *it* to the Levite, the stranger, the fatherless, and the widow, so that they may eat within your gates and be filled, [13]then you shall say before the Lord your God: 'I have removed the holy *tithe* from *my* house, and also have given them to the Levite, the stranger, the fatherless, and the widow, according to all Your commandments which You have commanded me; I have not transgressed Your commandments, nor have I forgotten *them*.

The stranger learned the Word of God and was expected to adhere to it: Deuteronomy 31:12 Gather the people together, men and women and little ones, and the stranger who *is* within your gates, that they may hear and that they may learn to fear the Lord your God and carefully observe all the words of this law, [13]and *that* their children, who have not known it, may hear and learn to fear the Lord your God as long as you live in the land which you cross the Jordan to possess."

The key then is to be converted: Matthew 18:2 Then Jesus called a little child to Him, set him in the midst of them, [3]and said, "Assuredly, I say to you, unless you are converted and become as little children, you will by no means enter the kingdom of heaven." The character of little children is that when they hear the firm word of mom or especially dad, they immediately obey their voice. Not so

*The Elephants In The Room!*

with the ancient Hebrew and not so with today's church on nearly every issue; so-called race is but one.

## Chapter 4
## The Wives of Abraham

To further illustrate the absurdity of separation in the body of Christ along so-called racial lines, consider The Genealogy of Christ. There are only four women (Matthew 1:1-6) mentioned in Christ's forty-two generational lineage over about 1050 years using 25 years as a generation marker; 840 years using 20 years as a generation marker. None of the women were of the House of Israel. Interestingly enough is the fact that Sarah didn't make the genealogical cut, who was barren for 90 years prior to miraculously giving birth to the Isaac.

Since Christ's genealogy begins with Abraham, we should first take a look at the three women the bible recognizes as his wives, and their racial component as represented by scripture. First and foremost it important recognize that Abraham was Syrian. Genesis 24 makes this very clear when Abraham makes his most trusted slave swear to find a wife for Isaac. Genesis 24:2 "So Abraham said to the oldest servant of his house, who ruled over all that he had, 'Please, put your hand under my thigh, ³and I will make you swear by the Lord, the God of heaven and the God of the earth, that you will not take a wife for my son from the daughters of the Canaanites, among whom I dwell; ⁴but you shall go to my country and to my family, and take a wife for my son Isaac.'"

Genesis 25:20 teaches that "Isaac was forty years old when he took Rebekah as wife, the daughter of Bethuel the Syrian of Padan Aram, the sister of Laban the Syrian." Bethuel was Abraham's nephew. Genesis 22:23 "And Bethuel begot Rebekah. These eight Milcah bore to Nahor, Abraham's brother." Obviously, God wanted the readers of His Word to know the truth, that being that Abraham's family were all Syrians. Why else would He tell us that both father and son were Syrian in the same sentence?

Consider Deuteronomy 26:5 "And you shall answer and say before the Lord your God: 'My father *was* a Syrian, about to perish, and he went down to Egypt and dwelt there, few in number; and there he became a nation, great, mighty, and populous." Again, the slave was sent to Abraham's country and to his family who were

## A Ernest Endeavor

Syrians, who are probably from the line of Shem (Noah's youngest son), through Aram, one of Shem's four sons. For the record, the "servant" uses the phrase "my master" 19 times (Genesis 24) when referring to Abraham. Clearly, the man saw himself as a slave even though translators used the word "servant."

Sarah, too, was of Syrian paternity. Abraham said in Genesis 20:12, "But indeed *she is* truly my sister. She *is* the daughter of my father, but not the daughter of my mother; and she became my wife." When Abraham left Haran (Genesis 12:5), didn't they have some Syrian women working for them? The Egyptians and the Syrians must have looked similar at that time. Why else would Sarah choose Hagar, an Egyptian, the father of whom is Ham, as a surrogate mother and second wife of Abraham?

Wouldn't Sarah want her child to resemble her even if produced by another woman? Is it possible that a huge number of barren white women, desperate to have children, given the choice, choose black women as their surrogates? Anything's possible. But it seems highly unlikely to me. It's nonsensical to think Sarah and Hagar were not of the same hue; especially since Hagar is of the seed of Egypt and Egypt is of the seed of Ham. Sarah probably elevated Hagar from maidservant to second wife—a significant promotion with full honors, no doubt, because they could pass for relatives. In the end, they were in fact blood relatives—distant cousins because Ham was the older brother of Shem.

As a brief aside, consider what Zipporah and her sisters said of Moses when he rescued them from bulling shepherds. Exodus 2:16 "Now the priest of Midian had seven daughters. And they came and drew water, and they filled the troughs to water their father's flock. [17] Then the shepherds came and drove them away; but Moses stood up and helped them, and watered their flock. [18] When they came to Reuel their father, he said, "How *is it that* you have come so soon today?" [19] And they said, "An Egyptian delivered us from the hand of the shepherds, and he also drew enough water for us and watered the flock." It's unlikely that Moses, being a Levite, told them he was an Egyptian, given that he was a fugitive from Egyptian justice. Assuming Moses did tell them he was an Egyptian, wouldn't that provoke more questions. For example, why would an Egyptian leave a rich and knowledgeable culture to gallivant with Bedouins? The simple answer is that the Midianite women had seen Egyptians and Moses easily passed for one. For the record, Midian was the son of Abraham—the Syrian.

Keturah, Abraham's third wife, was also of the seed of Ham being a native of Canaan, where Abraham lived. Genesis 25:1 "Abraham again took a wife, and her name *was* Keturah. [2]And she bore him Zimran, Jokshan, Medan, Midian, Ishbak, and Shuah. [3]Jokshan begot Sheba and Dedan. And the sons of Dedan were Asshurim, Letushim, and Leummim. [4]And the sons of Midian *were* Ephah, Epher, Hanoch, Abidah, and Eldaah. All these *were* the children of Keturah." Keturah must have been a very young woman compared to her husband who by this time was at least one-hundred-forty-years-old.

Acts 17:25 "Nor is He worshiped with men's hands, as though He needed anything, since He gives to all life, breath, and all things. [26]And He has made from one blood every nation of men to dwell on all the face of the earth, and has determined their preappointed times and the boundaries of their dwellings, [27]so that they should seek the Lord, in the hope that they might grope for

Him and find Him, though He is not far from each one of us." Abraham, the father of faith, had two wives who were born through the seed of Ham. This was somewhat of a prelude to the four women in Christ's lineage—race was not and is not a factor in the mind of God. After all, he made all in Adam.

## Chapter 5
## Four Very Special Women

Of the four women mentioned in Christ's lineage, the first was Tamar, a Canaanite, Judah's daughter-in-law, who also bore his twin children—Perez & Zerah (Genesis 38). The Canaanites were the grandchildren of Ham, the second son of Noah: Genesis 10:6 "The sons of Ham *were* Cush (Ethiopia), Mizraim (Egypt), Put (Libya), and Canaan. [15]Canaan begot Sidon his firstborn, and Heth; [16]the Jebusite, the Amorite, and the Girgashite; [17]the Hivite, the Arkite, and the Sinite; [18]the Arvadite, the Zemarite, and the Hamathite. Afterward the families of the Canaanites were dispersed. [19]And the border of the Canaanites was from Sidon as you go toward Gerar, as far as Gaza; then as you go toward Sodom, Gomorrah, Admah, and Zeboiim, as far as Lasha. [20]These *were* the sons of Ham, according to their families, according to their languages, in their lands *and* in their nations."

*The Elephants In The Room!*

It's amazing that even today, people within the church refuse to recognize Egypt, Libya, and the middle eastern people as coming through the seed of Ham. It's absolutely stunning that with the exception of South Africa, and those areas mentioned heretofore, the rest of Africa is attributed to Ham as if the Arabs, the Phoenicians, the Sidonians, the Lebanese, and the people of Nineveh are not Ham. Note that God is, and has always been, interested in saving all the grandchildren of Noah, the man He set aside for that very purpose. Christ came to save the world, did he not? With all of this biblical history, how then does today's church continue to ignore and deny their true brothers and sisters begotten by the Spirit of God. Romans 8:8 "So then, those who are in the flesh cannot please God. ⁹But you are not in the flesh but in the Spirit, if indeed the Spirit of God dwells in you. Now if anyone does not have the Spirit of Christ, he is not His."

The second woman was Rahab, the prostitute, who lived in Jericho, a seemingly impregnable fortress in the land of Canaan (Joshua 2:1-3; 6:17,23). Salmon married Rahab and she give birth to Boaz, the great-grandfather of David the king. It's important to note

## A Ernest Endeavor

that had the children of Israel gone into the promised land when the twelve spies returned, two Promised Land generations would not have been conceived. God had given the children of Israel orders to kill all the inhabitants of the Promised Land: Deuteronomy 7:16 "Also you shall destroy all the peoples whom the Lord your God delivers over to you; your eye shall have no pity on them; nor shall you serve their gods, for that *will be* a snare to you." Joshua 6:21 "And they utterly destroyed all that *was* in the city, both man and woman, young and old, ox and sheep and donkey, with the edge of the sword. [22] But Joshua had said to the two men who had spied out the country, "Go into the harlot's house, and from there bring out the woman and all that she has, as you swore to her." [23] And the young men who had been spies went in and brought out Rahab, her father, her mother, her brothers, and all that she had. So they brought out all her relatives and left them outside the camp of Israel."

If the children of Israel had entered the Promised Land when they were supposed to, Rahab may not have been born as prostitutes are usually younger women. If she was even a year old when they was supposed to enter the Promised Land, she would have been forty-one by the time they reached Jericho. She was probably in her twenties by the time Israel arrived. While Israel marched around the mountain for forty years, life in Jericho continued on as it always had. Other than Rahab, the inhabitants of Jericho probably never realized they had received forty years of mercy due to Israel's unbelief. Rahab and all of Jericho knew who the Israelites were and that they were being led by the God who defeated Egypt (Joshua 2:8-13). Having known the history of the children of Israel in Egypt, the people of Jericho didn't take advantage of the extended mercy with the exception of one lone prostitute, a daughter of Ham by way of Canaan.

The third woman was Ruth, a Moabitess. The Moabites are the incestuous children of Lot (Abraham's nephew), and his two daughters, intentionally conceived after they fled from the fire and brimstone God rained down on Sodom. Genesis 19:30 "Then Lot went up out of Zoar and dwelt in the mountains, and his two daughters were with him; for he was afraid to dwell in Zoar. And he and his two daughters dwelt in a cave. [31] Now the firstborn said to the younger, "Our father *is* old, and *there is* no man on the earth to come in to us as is the custom of all the earth. ³²Come, let us make our father drink wine, and we will lie with him, that we may preserve the lineage of our father." ³³So they made their father drink wine that night. And the firstborn went in and lay with her father, and he did not know when she lay down or when she arose. ³⁴It happened on the next day that the firstborn said to the younger, "Indeed I lay with my father last night; let us make him drink wine tonight also, and you go in *and* lie with him, that we may preserve the lineage of our father." ³⁵Then they made their father drink wine that night also. And the younger arose and lay with him, and he did not know when she lay down or when she arose. ³⁶Thus both the daughters of Lot were with child by their father. ³⁷The firstborn bore a son and called his name Moab; he *is* the father of the Moabites to this day. ³⁸And the younger, she also bore a son and called his name Ben-Ammi; he *is* the father of the people of Ammon to this day."

The fourth woman in Christ's linage was Bathsheba, a Hittite, who were one of the nations to be systematically removed, by way of death, from the Promised Land (Genesis 15:20; II Samuel 11:1-6). The bible makes it clear that Tamar, Rahab, and Bathsheba were sexually immoral women, which is important to note because Jesus, being a descendant of the incestuous Tamar, the harlotry of Rahab, and the adulterous Bathsheba, came to save sinners from the wrath to come. One may find it interesting that these three women were the distant cousins of Shem, as they too were the descendants of Ham, the second son of Noah, the father of Canaan, Egypt, Libya, and numerous other African and Middle Eastern peoples (Genesis 10:6-20). So then we see that Jesus, the Lamb of God, had come through the line of David, the son of Abraham, to save the entire world.

A Ernest Endeavor

# Chapter 6
# A Kingdom Divided

With few exceptions, the mothers of the begotten are not mentioned by name in biblical genealogies, but in Jesus' lineage four women were. Why? Probably for such a time as this. A time when some of the family of God forgets John 3:16 and what it truly means. Most Christians haven't forgotten John 3:16 (For God so loved the world that He gave His only begotten Son, that whoever believes in Him should not perish but have everlasting life) and they know *exactly* what it means.

And yet they reject the Word of Almighty God because they do not fear him when it comes to so-called "race." When there's no fear of God, it's easy to ignore the following scriptures: Jeremiah 5:22 "'Do you not fear me?' says the Lord. 'Will you not tremble at My presence, Who have placed the sand as the bound of the sea, By a perpetual decree, that it cannot pass beyond it? And though its waves toss to and fro, Yet they cannot prevail; Though they roar, yet they cannot pass over it.'"

Leviticus 19:17a 'You shall not hate your brother in your heart (mind)."

John 13:34 "A new commandment I give to you, that you love one another; as I have loved you, that you also love one another. 35 By this all will know that you are My disciples, if you have love for one another."

Further, because the church still accepts and embraces the Jim Crow separate but equal construct, the church is divided, which Christ warned against.

Matthew 12:25 But Jesus knew their thoughts, and said to them: "Every kingdom divided against itself is brought to desolation, and every city or house divided against itself will not stand." Jesus explained this further in verse 30a when he said, "He who is not with Me is against Me."

Matthew 22:34 But when the Pharisees heard that He had silenced the Sadducees, they gathered together. [35] Then one of them, a lawyer, asked *Him a question,* testing Him, and saying, [36] "Teacher, which *is* the great commandment in the law?" ³⁷Jesus said to him, "'You shall love the Lord your God with all your heart, with all your soul, and with all your mind.' ³⁸This is *the* first and great commandment. ³⁹And *the* second *is* like it: 'You shall love your neighbor as yourself.' ⁴⁰On these two commandments hang all the Law and the Prophets."

I've asked numerous Christians, black and white, "Will there be Jim Crow in heaven?" Some said, "I don't know. Others said, "Yes, I think so." Others said, "That's a tough one." There is but one right answer to the posed question. No, there will not be Jim Crow in heaven.

The questions were not posed during the tumultuous 1960s, but after the events of 911, a time when many people of the United States were supposedly coming together. There was standing room only in churches throughout the country the Sunday after 911. But fear, and the looming advent of the great white throne judgment (Revelation 20:11) was not a true catalyst for salvation. And the people dispersed again. Every man lived again according to the dictates of his own heart (Jeremiah 16:12; 18:12; 23:17).

*The Elephants In The Room!*

If there's any doubt that all the saints of God will be in heaven together, John puts it to rest with his vision. Revelation 7:9 "After these things I looked, and behold, a great multitude which no one could number, of all nations, tribes, peoples, and tongues, standing before the throne and before the Lamb, clothed with white robes, with palm branches in their hands, [10] and crying out with a loud voice, saying, "Salvation *belongs* to our God who sits on the throne, and to the Lamb!"

## Chapter 7
## Excuses

The fact that professing Christians didn't know there wouldn't be Jim Crow in heaven, which by the way is a universal memory verse for most believers (John 3:16), tells us exactly where the church is as a nation within a nation. Having heard their answers, I posed another question. Is there more than one Christ? The responses were quick and definitive. "No. There's only one Jesus." I then posed yet another question: Since Jim Crow won't be allowed in heaven, why does the body of Christ allow it on earth?

Some looked befuddled and said, "I don't know. Others said, "There are some integrated churches." Others said, "We're culturally different." There's some truth in those answers, but their answers don't negate the oneness of spirit the Holy Ghost brought on the Day of Pentecost, do they? Some said, "It's the music. We like different styles of music." That's true too. But it also negates "the assembling of ourselves together" (Hebrews 10:25) command doesn't it? Or did the writer of Hebrews mean, assemble yourselves together along the color line. Black Christians make sure you all stay with Christians of your likeness. Whites Christians, make sure you all do the same.

Is this not premeditated division? And if it's premeditated, isn't it sinful and a direct violation of Hebrews 10:25? And if it is sinful, why doesn't this disturb and sting the conscience of the body of Christ as a collective? Why hasn't the body of Christ repented in more than 400 years of separation, one from another, in the United States? Consider James 4:17 "Therefore, to him who knows to do good and does not do *it*, to him it is sin."

If the church is indeed the body of Christ, why is the church fine with this? The Holy Scripture is true where it says, "For they are not all Israel who are of Israel (Romans 9:6b)." In other words, perhaps the church is a shell of its former self. By the way, 'its former self' is a reference to the Day of Pentecost, not the Pilgrims landing on Plymouth Rock.

## A Ernest Endeavor

Consider Acts 2:5 "And there were dwelling in Jerusalem Jews, devout men, from every nation under heaven. ⁶And when this sound occurred, the multitude came together, and were confused, because everyone heard them speak in his own language. ⁷Then they were all amazed and marveled, saying to one another, "Look, are not all these who speak Galileans? ⁸And how *is it that* we hear, each in our own language in which we were born? ⁹Parthians and Medes and Elamites, those dwelling in Mesopotamia, Judea and Cappadocia, Pontus and Asia, ¹⁰Phrygia and Pamphylia, Egypt and the parts of Libya adjoining Cyrene, visitors from Rome, both Jews and proselytes, ¹¹Cretans and Arabs—we hear them speaking in our own tongues the wonderful works of God." ¹²So they were all amazed and perplexed, saying to one another, "Whatever could this mean?"

If the church is a shell of itself, and it is, perhaps the practitioners of Christianity no longer accept long held doctrines as immutable truth, and haven't for a very long time. Malachi 3:6a "For I *am* the Lord, I do not change." If the Lord doesn't change, who changed? There's been a decisive change of heart in the body of Christ despite many warnings and Old Testament illustrations. But alas, Old Testament teachings, for the most part, have been thoroughly rejected or ignored because of the era of grace.

Perhaps the greatest rejection of Old Testament scripture can be found in Deuteronomy 6:6 "And these words which I command you today shall be in your heart. [7] You shall teach them diligently to your children, and shall talk of them when you sit in your house, when you walk by the way, when you lie down, and when you rise up." This command has been routinely ignored in Christian households in the United States. Someone might say, "That's a bold statement. Where's the proof of this?" The minds of many Christians have been fed a steady diet of deceit which has led to spiritual senility. Consider Matthew 15:18 "But those things which proceed out of the mouth come from the heart, and they defile a man. [19] For out of the heart proceed evil thoughts, murders, adulteries, fornications, thefts, false witness, blasphemies."

Paul admonished the church with the following exhortation, "Examine yourselves, whether ye be in the faith; prove your own selves. Know ye not your own selves, how that Jesus Christ is in you, except ye be reprobates (II Corinthians 13:5 KJV)? The church cannot see itself because it refuses to look into the mirror—the Holy Scriptures. Therefore, there's isn't much heart reflection. Jeremiah 17:9 "The heart *is* deceitful above all *things,* And desperately wicked; Who can know it? [10] I, the Lord, search the heart, *I* test the mind, Even to give every man according to his ways, According to the fruit of his doings.

Deuteronomy 6:10-12 hits the bullseye for what's happened to the modern-day church in the United States of America. "So it shall be, when the Lord your God brings you into the land of which He swore to your fathers, to Abraham, Isaac, and Jacob, to give you large and beautiful cities which you did not build, [11] houses full of all good things, which you did not fill, hewn-out wells which you did not dig, vineyards and olive trees which you did not plant—when you have eaten and are full— [12] *then* beware, lest you forget the Lord who brought you out of the land of Egypt, from the house of bondage." But forgetting the Lord began as far back as the colonial period. The early Christians planted the seeds of forgetting God and now the United States is reaping what was sown hundreds of years ago.

## Chapter 8

## An Unholy Harvest

The physical eye is designed to see everything outside the body. The Spiritual eye is designed to see everything within the heart with the aid of scripture as The Holy Spirit illuminates the regenerated mind. John 14:15 "If you love Me, keep My commandments. [16] And I will pray the Father, and He will give you another Helper, that He may abide with you forever— [17] the Spirit of truth, whom the world cannot receive, because it neither sees Him nor knows Him; but you know Him, for He dwells with you and will be in you." St. John 14:26 "But the Helper, the Holy Spirit, whom the Father will send in My name, He will teach you all things, and bring to your remembrance all things that I said to you."

Due to the mismanagement of the colonial church and its rejection of absolute truth, the modern-day church is filled with false teachers, blind guides, and outright charlatans. For discernment, the church must return to the unadulterated truth found in the following scriptures. Matthew 15:14c "And if the blind leads the blind, both will fall into a ditch." The corruption is on the inside and can only be controlled by The Holy Spirit (Ephesians 5:18c). The heart and the mind are virtually inseparable. The heart therefore has to be shielded from as much corruption as possible. Galatians 5:13 "For you, brethren, have been called to liberty; only do not *use* liberty as an opportunity for the flesh, but through love serve one another." Proverbs 4:23 "Keep your heart with all diligence for out of it flow the issues of life." Ephesians 4:23 "and be renewed in the spirit of your mind, [24] and that you put on the new man which was created according to God, in true righteousness and holiness." Philippians 2:5 "Let this mind be in you which was also in Christ Jesus."

For more proof that the church has lost its way, consider the scripturally sound doctrines the church has openly rejected and what the church has now accepted as truth that has no scriptural foundation whatsoever. Some might ask, "To what doctrines do you refer?" My response is this: "If I have to tell you . . . if you don't already know . . . then we're far worse off than I thought." The rejection of the written Word of God is what led the church's spiritual forefathers to near oblivion and in numerous cases a return to captivity, was it not?

Nevertheless the 7-ton elephant in the room isn't just the self-imposed Jim Crow segregation within the body of Christ, it's the unabated dislike and in some cases hatred between black Christians and white Christians that's been building for more than 20 generations. Most of the Christian Community is either blind to this flagrant hypocrisy or they see it, recognize it for what it is, but refuse to acknowledge it by figuratively closing their eyes, rejecting the following scriptures.

1 John 4:20 "If someone says, 'I love God,' and hates his brother, he is a liar; for he who does not love his brother whom he has seen, how can he love God whom he has not seen? 21 And this commandment we have from Him: that he who loves God must love his brother also." Both the black "church" and the white "church" seem to be okay with this lethal "arrangement". Ignoring these straightforward scriptures is destroying Christianity. As the light of

the church fades into darkness, as its devoted membership wanes, so is its influence in every institution of the United States.

The church has forgotten Galatians 5:9 "A little leaven leavens the whole lump." Members of both churches tell themselves, "I don't hate my black brother. Or I don't hate my white brother." All of this while flagrantly violating Hebrews 10:25. All of this while forgetting that this is a spiritual thing, "For we wrestle not with flesh and blood . . ." (Ephesians 6:12). All of this while exhibiting a duality of mind that is contrary to the precepts, statutes, and laws of the God who sent his Son to be a propitiation.

Hebrews 2:17 "Therefore, in all things He had to be made like *His* brethren, that He might be a merciful and faithful High Priest in things *pertaining* to God, to make propitiation for the sins of the people." 1 John 2:2 "And He Himself is the propitiation for our sins, and not for ours only but also for the whole world." 1 John 4:10 "In this is love, not that we loved God, but that He loved us and sent His Son *to be* the propitiation for our sins."

Because the church has forgotten these principles and God's sovereign right to rule his people as He sees fit, the church is conflicted, and losing a spiritual battle it can ill afford to lose. Losing this spiritual battle puts the church's children in danger. Consider Hosea 4:6 "My people are destroyed for lack of knowledge. Because you have rejected knowledge, I also will reject you from being priest for Me; Because you have forgotten the law of your God, I also forget your children."

A Ernest Endeavor

## CHAPTER 9
## LOST IN TRANSLATION

Due to the church's self-imposed blindness, it's being outflanked and overrun by devil worshipers who do not appear as such. II Corinthians 11:13 "For such *are* false apostles, deceitful workers, transforming themselves into apostles of Christ. ¹⁴And no wonder! For Satan himself transforms himself into an angel of light. ¹⁵Therefore *it is* no great thing if his ministers also transform themselves into ministers of righteousness, whose end will be according to their works."

For clarification's sake, there are three kinds of devil worshippers—none are obvious. They don't generally look like a fully possessed Linda Blair from the film, *The Exorcist. The Matrix* is a more apt visual depiction. They appear to be regular people, but they are far from it.

The first kind of devil worshipper think of themselves as good people and by man's standards they are. However, the standard according to Christ is far higher—so high in fact that it's impossible for man. A single verse in The Sermon On The Mount shows the impossibility to those that have judged themselves as righteous or good. Matthew 5:48 "Therefore you shall be perfect, just as your Father in heaven is perfect." There are those within church leadership, theologians, scholars, who believe that the word "perfect" means maturity. This is an example of demonic influence— the lowering of God's righteous way in order for man to reach it while simultaneously eliminating the need for Christ.

Interpreting the word "perfect" as maturity would have to apply to both words in the sentence. On the one hand, God is perfect. No Christian would have a problem with that. No Christian would have a problem with Christians striving for the highest form of maturity because man cannot perfect himself. Another problem is the translation itself. If the Greek word for "perfect" is indeed maturity, why did the translator(s) use the word perfect? And having used the word "perfect" when referring to God, why use it when referring to man in the same sentence? Both words would have the same meaning, right? Any other interpretation would then reduce a

A Ernest Endeavor

HOLY and RIGHTEOUS God to a mature God, not a perfect God, right? That makes no sense logically and more important, it makes no sense spiritually.

Christ had a direct, unmistakable message to the "good" people of the world; a message that needed no interpretation and no translation; a message that lets the self-righteous person know that they are in just as much danger of the damnation to hell as any person thought of as a sure fire candidate for the lake of fire. Mark 10:18 "So Jesus said to him, "Why do you call Me good? No one *is* good but One, *that is,* God." In other words, even people who are considered good need their sins covered by Christ. James 2:10 For whoever shall keep the whole law, and yet stumble in one *point,* he is guilty of all. Romans 10:2 "For I bear them witness that they have a zeal for God, but not according to knowledge. ³For they being ignorant of God's righteousness, and seeking to establish their own righteousness, have not submitted to the righteousness of God. ⁴For Christ *is* the end of the law for righteousness to everyone who believes." Being good is not good enough because man can never be good enough on his own. He can feel good about himself, and end up in hell with those who sold their souls.

The second kind of devil worshipper knows they've sold their souls to Satan and have been well compensated for doing so. Many of which are firmly ensconced in influential positions in Hollywood, politics, mainstream media, education, religious institutions, and various billion dollar industries. The rank and file who work for these powerbrokers have no idea they're being led astray—in fact to their own destruction. Matthew 12:30 Jesus said, "He who is not with Me is against Me, and he who does not gather with Me scatters abroad."

The third and perhaps the most dangerous devil worshippers are in the church's hierarchy itself. Consider the debate Jesus had with the church leaders of his day. John 8:37 "I know that you are Abraham's descendants, but you seek to kill Me, because My word has no place in you. [38] I speak what I have seen with My Father, and you do what you have seen with your father." [39] They answered and said to Him, "Abraham is our father." Jesus said to them, "If you were Abraham's children, you would do the works of

Abraham. ⁴⁰But now you seek to kill Me, a Man who has told you the truth which I heard from God. Abraham did not do this. ⁴¹You do the deeds of your father."

Then they said to Him, "We were not born of fornication; we have one Father—God." ⁴²Jesus said to them, "If God were your Father, you would love Me, for I proceeded forth and came from God; nor have I come of Myself, but He sent Me. ⁴³Why do you not understand My speech? Because you are not able to listen to My word. ⁴⁴You are of *your* father the devil, and the desires of your father you want to do. He was a murderer from the beginning, and does not stand in the truth, because there is no truth in him. When he speaks a lie, he speaks from his own *resources,* for he is a liar and the father of it. ⁴⁵But because I tell the truth, you do not believe Me. ⁴⁶Which of you convicts Me of sin? And if I tell the truth, why do you not believe Me? ⁴⁷He who is of God hears God's words; therefore you do not hear, because you are not of God."

Imagine that! Jesus told the chief priests, the pharisees, and the scribes, men who were "experts" of biblical texts to their faces that they were not of God. Later, in Matthew 23:27 Jesus compared

*The Elephants In The Room!*

the church leadership of his day to mausoleums with a fresh coat of white paint when he said, "Woe to you, scribes and Pharisees, hypocrites! For you are like whitewashed tombs which indeed appear beautiful outwardly, but inside are full of dead *men's* bones and all uncleanness."

A Ernest Endeavor

# CHAPTER 10
# MAJOR ENGAGEMENTS

And so there is a fierce and bloody spiritual battle going on within the churches in America for the souls of men. Some of the household of God will respond by saying, "for the battle is not yours, but God's (II Chronicles 20:15). My question is this: But didn't He (God) give explicit orders to Israel to do the fighting? Did he not also say, "Occupy until I come (Luke 19:13 KJV)? The church is to be an occupying force for the kingdom of God. It is to be salt and light in a world getting darker by the second.

Matthew 5:13 "You are the salt of the earth; but if the salt loses its flavor, how shall it be seasoned? It is then good for nothing but to be thrown out and trampled underfoot by men. [14]"You are the light of the world. A city that is set on a hill cannot be hidden. [15]Nor do they light a lamp and put it under a basket, but on a lampstand, and it gives light to all *who are* in the house. [16]Let your light so shine before men, that they may see your good works and glorify your Father in heaven."

Unfortunately, the church is at the precipice of being neither salt nor light due to the never-ending division in the house of God. Others use I Timothy 4:1 "Now the Spirit expressly says that in latter times some will depart from the faith, giving heed to deceiving spirits and doctrines of demons, ²speaking lies in hypocrisy, having their own conscience seared with a hot iron." If the 21$^{st}$ century is the last days, what prevented the church from obeying the scriptures in the 20$^{th}$ century or the 15$^{th}$ century for that matter. Why stop there? This nonchalant attitude could be used in any era, could it not? But, if the church truly believes it is the last days, why are its members still striving to get ahead, preparing for a favorable future like those who are not of the household of faith?

This hassle-free attitude has cost the church every major engagement with the enemy, much like the forefathers of the faith who did not want to conqueror the promised land—never mind that God warned them that peace treaties would be their undoing. Exodus 34:12 "Take heed to yourself, lest you make a covenant with the inhabitants of the land where you are going, lest it be a snare in your midst."

"Those who cannot remember the past are condemned to repeat it." The quote has been credited to philosopher George Santayana. A penetrating look at the church in American history could possibly shed some much-needed light on how the "Christian Nation" lost the battle for its country to homosexuality.

The first engagement the church lost in The New World is the oneness of the body of Christ by allowing slavery in the colonies to legally flourish from 1619 to 1863. Think about that. That's two-hundred and forty-four years of vassalage, plus decades of legal segregation and The Jim Crow Laws that the white "church" seemed to be fine with, blatantly ignoring three guiding scriptures in the bible.

The first guiding scripture has been dubbed, The Golden Rule. "Therefore, whatever you want men to do to you, do also to them, for this is the Law and the Prophets" (Matthew 7:12). The second guiding scripture is the second greatest commandment. "And the second, like *it, is* this: 'You shall love your neighbor as yourself.' There is no other commandment greater than these" (Mark 12:31).

*The Elephants In The Room!*

The third guiding scripture can be found in Exodus 21:16 "He who kidnaps a man and sells him, or if he is found in his hand, shall surely be put to death." While the following verse specifically points to the children of Israel, let's not forget that I've already cited the scriptures that teach there is to be one law for Israel and the stranger among them.

Deuteronomy 24:7 If a man is found kidnapping any of his brethren of the children of Israel, and mistreats him or sells him, then that kidnapper shall die; and you shall put away the evil from among you. 1 Timothy 1:8 But we know that the law *is* good if one uses it lawfully, [9]knowing this: that the law is not made for a righteous person, but for *the* lawless and insubordinate, for *the* ungodly and for sinners, for *the* unholy and profane, for murderers of fathers and murderers of mothers, for manslayers, [10]for fornicators, for sodomites, **for kidnappers**, for liars, for perjurers, and if there is any other thing that is contrary to sound doctrine, [11]according to the glorious gospel of the blessed God which was committed to my trust.

A Ernest Endeavor

# Chapter 11
# The Golden Rule

For those who *now* think this book is about American Slavery, it isn't. And it never was. Colonial slavery is mentioned because it points to when and where the rejection of the sovereignty of God began. It was blatant hypocrisy to introduce slaves to Jesus as both Lord & Savior while at the same time treating him as if he's an enemy when according to the Word of God, he became a brother when he accepted Christ. And as a brother of the faith, he should have been treated with all the rights and blessing of becoming a son of God.

Ephesians 4:1 "I, therefore, the prisoner of the Lord, beseech you to walk worthy of the calling with which you were called, ²with all lowliness and gentleness, with longsuffering, bearing with one another in love, ³endeavoring to keep the unity of the Spirit in the bond of peace. ⁴*There is* one body and one Spirit, just as you were called in one hope of your calling; ⁵one Lord, one faith, one baptism; [6]one God and Father of all, who *is* above all, and through all, and in you all."

To the above scriptures, some might say, "Well, the slaveholders were not Christians." Question: Assuming slaveholders were not Christians, where were the true Christians while all the savagery and debauchery was going on? And if slaveholders were not in fact Christians, when did North America adopt the moniker, Christian Nation? More important, when was it practiced consistently? It wasn't.

Nevertheless, there were some true believers in North America during the slavery era and they were zealous for righteousness according to biblical standards—at least early on. Consider the following quote from historian Joel Augustus Rogers in his life's work, Sex and Race Vol. II, 1942, page 155. "In 1630 comes the first record of a white man and a negro woman in Virginia. It reads: 'September 17, 1630. Hugh Davis to be soundly whipped before an assembly of Negroes and others for abusing himself to the dishonor of God and the shame of Christians by defiling his body in lying with a Negro.' In 1640 comes the second record, but not necessarily the second offense—much of the early Virginia records were lost. It reads: '1640 Robert Sweet to do penance in church, according to the laws of England for getting a Negro woman in child, and the woman whipt.' The third mention of miscegenation in the Virginia records is 1662, and provides for the disposition of mulatto children born in the colony. It reads, Article XII 'Children got by an Englishman upon a Negro woman shall be bond or free according to the condition of the mother and if any Christian shall commit fornication with a Negro man or woman he shall pay double the fines of the former act.'"

Clearly there were Christians who believed in biblical principles, but over time, there was a distinct reversal of morality. Whipping was the original sentence doled out to white Christian men who fornicated with black women. Ten years later the sentence was repealed and transferred to the black female, who in all likelihood was a slave. The Christian man did penance in the church and the woman was whipped. It didn't take long for Christian morality to severely diminish.

*The Elephants In The Room!*

The practice of Christianity has been a joke from nearly its beginning in North America, particularly where blacks were concerned. The precedent for seeing blacks as neighbors was set in the 17th century and has continued into the 21st century. The church eventually saw blacks the same way non-Christians saw them. They were chattel, not fellow brothers in Christ. They weren't even Christian neighbors which required certain practices mentioned heretofore.

Is it any wonder the following scripture is still being largely ignored within the church by Christian separatists today? Luke 10:30 "Then Jesus answered and said: 'A certain *man* went down from Jerusalem to Jericho, and fell among thieves, who stripped him of his clothing, wounded *him,* and departed, leaving *him* half dead. [31] Now by chance a certain priest came down that road. And when he saw him, he passed by on the other side. [32] Likewise a Levite, when he arrived at the place, came and looked, and passed by on the other side. [33] But a certain Samaritan, as he journeyed, came where he was. And when he saw him, he had compassion. [34] So he went to *him* and bandaged his wounds, pouring on oil and wine; and he set him on his own animal, brought him to an inn, and took care of him. [35] On the next day, when he departed, he took out two denarii, gave *them* to the innkeeper, and said to him, 'Take care of him; and whatever more you spend, when I come again, I will repay you.' [36] So which of these three do you think was neighbor to him who fell among the thieves?' [37] And he said, 'He who showed mercy on him.' Then Jesus said to him, 'Go and do likewise.'"

Matthew 7:12 "Therefore, whatever you want men to do to you, do also to them, for this is the Law and the Prophets." The Golden Rule means absolutely nothing to Christians who approve of and practice Jim Crow in the 21$^{st}$ century, because it meant nothing 400 years ago at the installation of colonial slavery. For clarity's sake, the practice of Christianity was not restricted to Caucasians. The standards of Christianity are extremely high. Its namesake, for example, taught that it wasn't enough to love one's brother in the faith, but to love one's enemy who wasn't even a part of the Christian Community.

Consider the following scriptures: Matthew 5:43 "You have heard that it was said, 'You shall love your neighbor and hate your enemy.' ⁴⁴But I say to you, love your enemies, bless those who curse you, do good to those who hate you, and pray for those who spitefully use you and persecute you, ⁴⁵that you may be sons of your Father in heaven; for He makes His sun rise on the evil and on the good, and sends rain on the just and on the unjust. ⁴⁶For if you love those who love you, what reward have you? Do not even the tax collectors do the same? ⁴⁷And if you greet your brethren only, what do you do more *than others?* Do not even the tax collectors do so? ⁴⁸Therefore you shall be perfect, just as your Father in heaven is perfect."

Jesus made it clear that religious people are not necessarily his disciples. Matthew 7:21 "Not everyone who says to Me, 'Lord, Lord,' shall enter the kingdom of heaven, but he who does the will of My Father in heaven." He went on to say in Matthew 12:30a "He who is not with Me is against Me." Those are pretty sobering statements to members of the Christian faith.

Is it any wonder that the church has lost the sanctity of marriage, the sanctity of the womb, the sanctity of children by way of the public school system, and the sanctity of life itself? These gifts are intimately woven together to keep all of society accountable to God. They have all been inexplicably squandered. As a result, Christians are no longer safe in their own churches. The Enemy is going into their places of worship loaded for bear, blowing away its membership in the sanctuary on a whim. And still the church refuses to listen to their God who pleads with them to turn from their wicked ways.

  Isaiah 65:2 "I have stretched out My hands all day long to a rebellious people, Who walk in a way that is not good, According to their own thoughts." The church has become altogether deaf due to their incessant rebellion against the orders of a **HOLY** and **RIGHTEOUS** God to love one another. II Chronicles 7:14 "if My people who are called by My name will humble themselves, and pray and seek My face, and turn from their wicked ways, then I will hear from heaven, and will forgive their sin and heal their land." The healing of the United States is based on the Christian community turning from its wicked ways.

## CHAPTER 12
## SURGICAL COMA

In response to the contradiction within the church, what are the children of the devil doing? Are they satisfied with glorious victory after glorious victory? No! They're rolling over Christianity like the Third Reich rolled through Europe during WWII—nearly unopposed. And if the church doesn't awaken from its self-imposed surgical coma, it will soon find itself in concentration camps; or worse, in ovens, burning, yet living long enough to feel the excruciating fiery flame until it turns to dust. Some believers might say, "Shadrach, Meshach, and Abed-Nego survived the fiery flame during Nebuchadnezzar's time."

Agreed.

But all three of the Hebrew boys took a firm political stand for God's ways when it was unpopular, trusting Him to deliver them or not. When confronted, here's what the three boys said. Daniel 3:16 "Shadrach, Meshach, and Abed-Nego answered and said to the king, "O Nebuchadnezzar, we have no need to answer you in this matter. ⁷¹If that *is the case,* our God whom we serve is able to deliver us from the burning fiery furnace, and He will deliver *us* from your hand, O king. ¹⁸But if not, let it be known to you, O king, that we do not serve your gods, nor will we worship the gold image which you have set up."

If the church trusted in their God and not in Civil Rights Leaders and Civil Rights Legislation to right historical wrongs, I have no doubt that Christianity would still own the definition of marriage, life and the sanctity thereof, and the public-school system. Every civil wrong perpetrated by The United States Government, could have been handled by an organization that lauds itself as a Christian Country. The lack of true brotherly love turned brother against brother, both of whom rejected their God's clear counsel on all grievances within his household—and the cold war between the "black" Church and the "white" Church continues unabated.

The following scriptures have been wholly rejected at the micro and macro levels within the Christian community for hundreds, if not thousands of years. Matthew 18:15 "Moreover if your brother sins against you, go and tell him his fault between you and him alone. If he hears you, you have gained your brother. [16] But if he will not hear, take with you one or two more, that 'by the mouth of two or three witnesses every word may be established.' [17] And if he refuses to hear them, tell *it* to the church. But if he refuses even to hear the church, let him be to you like a heathen and a tax collector." The King James version, widely used in the United States was published more than four-hundred-years ago in the year 1611. The rejection of God's Word for four centuries is bringing the church to its knees.

In the meantime, while the church twiddles its collective thumbs, the children of the devil are fortifying their positions as they observed the church's generational hypocrisy. They're planning to take Christians out *period*. To devil worshippers, especially those of the self-righteous ilk, the influence of Christianity is the problem in "their" world. Because of Christianity, until the Obama presidency made it legal, homosexuals and lesbians could not engage in "holy matrimony". Lest we forget, marriage is a holy sacrament ordained by God himself, who both defined marriage and the sexual practices

## A Ernest Endeavor

therein (Hebrews 13:4). Prior to the Obama Administration, homosexuals and lesbians[1] had to willfully live in defiance of God's uncompromising word. For the record, former President Obama is a professing Christian[2].

---

[1] The Obama Legacy: The Legalization of Gay Marriage | by Emma McDonald | The Progressive Teen | Medium
[2] Obama says he became a Christian by choice - Los Angeles Times (latimes.com)

## Chapter 13
## Hypocrisy

For decades, the children of the devil listened to Christians talk out of both sides of their mouths, saying one thing, and doing another. They watched gleefully, no doubt taking notes, as Christians brazenly violated the Holy Scriptures, its laws, and the precepts of their Holy God (I Peter 1:16).

Having repeatedly broken many sacred trusts, the church has conveniently swept those same violations under the proverbial rug, covering their wicked ways with lies that salved what little conscience it had left. I'm sure the mouths of the children of the devil freely slobbered with anticipation as they watched Christian men and women flagrantly rebel against sexual abstinence, resulting in unwanted pregnancy.

This unholy happenstance then led many Christian women to places like Planned Parenthood to get their abortion on demand. "In a survey that was sponsored by the pregnancy center support organization Care Net, researchers from the Christian research group LifeWay found that about 70 percent of women who had an abortion self-identified as Christians[3], while 43 percent say they attended a Christian church at least once per month or more at the time they aborted their child."

Worse yet is that the church's sexual habits were and are being bequeathed to their unsuspecting offspring through their repeated acts of sexual illegality, which shackles generation after generation of Christians to the slavery of unholy sexual activity.

Since there was no real response by the church and its leadership to the practice of sexual misconduct in the body of Christ, other than shaming the women and girls who were with child, sexual corruption became acceptable under the pretenses of love; and all of that was fine and dandy. Is it any wonder that the children of the righteous do as those who reproduced them have done? The devil's children strategically observed the church's collective position on all

---

[3] (https://www.christianpost.com/news/70-of-women-who-get-abortions-identify-as-christians-survey-finds.html).

of this, and sang, "Zip-a-dee-doo-dah! We finally have 'em right where we want 'em!"

The children of the devil watched as members of the clergy raped little boys on a massive scale, turning them into unholy practitioners of the same. And still the church did little to nothing to stop it. There wasn't much, if any, outcry from practicing members and no church discipline whatsoever.

Consider I Corinthians 5:9 "I wrote to you in my epistle not to keep company with sexually immoral people. [10] Yet *I* certainly *did* not *mean* with the sexually immoral people of this world, or with the covetous, or extortioners, or idolaters, since then you would need to go out of the world. [11] But now I have written to you not to keep company with anyone named a brother, who is sexually immoral, or covetous, or an idolater, or a reviler, or a drunkard, or an extortioner—not even to eat with such a person. [12] For what *have* I *to do* with judging those also who are outside? Do you not judge those who are inside? [13] But those who are outside God judges. Therefore 'put away from yourselves the evil person.'"

A Ernest Endeavor

Perhaps that's why when men and boys are raped, not only in the penal system, but on America's streets[4], either people pretend like it isn't happening, or it's something to be laughed about instead of boldly pointing a finger at it and saying, "This is the FACE OF EVIL!" I Peter 4:17a "For the time has come for judgment to begin at the house of God."

Sadly, I've heard numerous women laughing about men being raped. Think about that for a minute. Those who are most vulnerable to rape, laugh when they hear jokes about men being raped. I can only guess that these women see nothing wrong with men being sexually assaulted—and so not only does the hypocrisy continue, it isn't confined to a specific sex.

I suppose that when the children of the devil saw Christianity in a weakened and vulnerable state, inches away from dying out altogether, they attacked their political institutions and changed the laws to favor them. The attacks were not a haphazard or spur of the moment thing. On the contrary, the attacks were coordinated,

---
[4] (http://cavemancircus.com/2018/11/13/male_rape_victim/)

concentrated, and diabolically cunning. Now that they are in charge and fully ensconced in the seats of supreme authority, wielding nearly unlimited power, they're planning to do (in reverse) what God ordered the children of Israel to do when they entered The Promised Land—annihilate Christians!

Why?

Christianity is the ultimate snare for unbelievers because it is the power of God to SALVATION to everyone who believes (Romans 1:16b). The last thing they want is another conversion like that of Saul who later became Paul (Acts 9).

## Chapter 14
## The Plot Thickens

As the church continues to forget its God (Hosea 4:6c), the devil's children are solidifying their positions in the education centers, surreptitiously programming the children of the believing and unbelieving worlds. They attend the same school systems, colleges, and universities. Indoctrination is the delivery apparatus used to supply spiritual, social, and ideological hemlock to future leaders with philosophies that contradict God's Word.

The concerted effort to brainwash the gray matter of the innocent has been going on for more than half a century, perhaps longer, through radio, television, movies, music, books, magazines, news networks, political persuasion and practically everything that exalts itself against the knowledge of God (II Corinthians 10:5). This process ensures that every year the indoctrinated run to the polls to vote for the very people who poisoned their minds, and in doing so, enslaved them.

The best slaves are those who don't know they're slaves, many of whom are African American Christians. They think they're free—but they're far from it. Many African American Christians are political sharecroppers with a Terminator's mentality—They can't be reasoned with and they absolutely will not stop voting against their own interests because their minds are in lockstep with the system that kidnapped them more than 400 years ago.

That same system introduced them to a counterfeit formulation of Christianity—one that was undeniably devoid of true freedom—physical, sociological, and most important, psychological. But the good news is an awakening is on the horizon—one that will keep them wide-awake for the foreseeable future, which just might make it possible to remove one of the elephants in the room.

One of the biggest elephants in the room is the alarming number of women teachers in the very same school systems engaging in repeated sexual activity with their male and female pupils (Hosea 4:6c). The illegality of statutory rape has not been a deterrent to the popular crime over the course of 30 years, perhaps longer as boys are not encouraged to report the abuse[5]. So common place is it that numerous websites have been built to expose the women who have been caught.

One particular woman in the Houston, Texas area was not only having sex regularly in her home with a male in the 8th grade, she claims that the boy's parents not only knew, but approved of the relationship, which resulted in pregnancy, and ultimately abortion. Can you see just how destructive the popular phrase, "Age is just a number," has been? The boy often spent the night at her home, but in the morning, she took him home[6], so he could take the bus to "school."

When the Christian community surrendered the schools and consequently the children (Hosea 4:6c), the nation was relinquished by default. After all, children are the future, right? The decline of social norms and civility was only a matter of time when the Ten Commandments and prayer were removed from schools

---

[5] Female Teachers as Sexual Predators | Psychology Today
[6] https://www.wnd.com/2014/08/39783/?

and replaced with atheism, socialism, and hedonism—the pursuit of pleasure and sensual self-indulgence.

The church has unquestionably given into whoredom—and not the women only. In fact, history proves that men are and have been the unmistakable trailblazers of debauchery for thousands of years. Therefore, it's impossible to have outright whores and courtesans unless men not only approve, but lead the way in the unholy endeavor. Hosea 4:14 "I will not punish your daughters when they commit harlotry, Nor your brides when they commit adultery; For the men themselves go apart with harlots, And offer sacrifices with a ritual harlot."

But the biggest elephant in the room is the proliferation of homosexuality in the church, wearing the garments of the priests, in the roles of head usher, deacon, choir director, choir member, minister of music, organist, pianist, lead guitarist, nurses aid, Sunday schoolteacher, security, and virtually every position in the building (I Corinthians 5:9-13). So prevalent is it in the church that the motion picture and music industries, including Hip-Hop and Gangsta Rap, have publicly embraced it—and it's there to stay.

A Ernest Endeavor

To illustrate just how effective the church's failure has been, they've persuaded much of Black Hollywood "to go along to get along." And they've greatly rewarded those who have yielded to the lucrative seduction with big budget films and television shows that prominently feature homosexuality and lesbianism. Shows like *Scandal*, *How to get away with Murder*, *Empire,* and the Oprah Winfrey Network's *Greenleaf* are standout leaders in the battle for the souls of black folk—all of this can be laid comfortably at the feet of the church and its embracing of Jim Crow[7] within its hallowed halls.

Blacks are now routinely winning Oscars, Golden Globes, Emmys, and Screen Actors Guild statues. The blockbuster film, *Black Panther*, which grossed more than 1.3 trillion dollars to date[8], and did not feature its usual staple of a wide variety of sexuality, probably would not have been achieved without the previously stated capitulation. However, the film is rife with mysticism and

---

[7] Matthew 12:25 But Jesus knew their thoughts, and said to them: "Every kingdom divided against itself is brought to desolation, and every city or house divided against itself will not stand.
[8] https://www.boxofficemojo.com

necromancy—the practice of communicating with dead people to learn more about the future.

Some people, in anger, might scream, "It's about time African Americans got their just due in Hollywood!" Agreed. But at what cost? The reality is this: Black folk define what's cool, not only in the United States, but throughout the world period. Being the definition of what's cool and acceptable is not a good thing if Black folk define evil as good. Consider what God put in the mouth of the prophet. Isaiah 5:20 "Woe to those who call evil good, and good evil; Who put darkness for light, and light for darkness; Who put bitter for sweet, and sweet for bitter!"

At some point, the elephant in the room must be seen for what it is—a monstrosity that's bringing the body of Christ to its collective knees. At some point, the so-called black church and the so-called white church must resolve petty and significant differences and conflicts and unify as Christ intended (John 17:11). Ironically, the homosexual community has shown Christians the way. Consider what they've accomplished over the course of 2 to 3 decades.

## A Ernest Endeavor

The homosexual community accomplished their goals while being a minority group. The National Gay and Lesbian Task Force estimates that Gays make up 3 to 8 percent of both sexes. Yet they're running rough-shod over the body of Christ due to nonresistance, but mainly due to the House of God being divided against itself while enthusiastically violating the prescribed dogma of abstinence detailed in the scriptures.

If the people of God do not confront the enormous elephants in the room directly and speedily, I have no doubt that the church will end up on the ash heap of history, much like its predecessor and older brother, Israel. Consider Jeremiah 18:7 "The instant I speak concerning a nation and concerning a kingdom, to pluck up, to pull down, and to destroy *it,* [8] if that nation against whom I have spoken turns from its evil, I will relent of the disaster that I thought to bring upon it.

"[9] And the instant I speak concerning a nation and concerning a kingdom, to build and to plant *it,* [10] if it does evil in My sight so that it does not obey My voice, then I will relent concerning the good with which I said I would benefit it." The latter is where the church is today, but it's not too late to reverse course.

Finally, this is what God has said about his chosen people: "For My people are foolish, They have not known Me. They are silly children. And they have no understanding. They are wise to do evil, But to do good they have no knowledge" (Jeremiah 4:22).

A Ernest Endeavor

# Preview of Book 2

## For Christians Only The Original Pimp!

# CHAPTER 1
# GOD IS UNFAIR

Given the title, Christian readers are probably thinking the author of this work isn't a true believer because he's being blasphemous from the outset. Non-Christians are saying, "Yeah, he's right. God isn't fair. Never was. Never will be." There are probably a lot of Christians, who for various reasons, wholeheartedly agree with non-Christians on how they truly see *their* God in the person of the anointed one, Jesus Christ.

Few Christians, if any, would ever say God is unfair aloud, but many think and believe it, especially women—believers and unbelievers alike. Believers often forget[9] that *their* God has access to the secret workings of their innermost being. They forget that He knows their thoughts[10].

I Samuel 16:[7] is an excellent example of this. "But the LORD said to Samuel, "Do not look at his appearance or at his physical stature, because I have refused him. For *the*

---

[9] As unbelievable as it may sound, it's possible that Christians never knew or perhaps never realized that God knows their thoughts.
[10] Genesis 6:[5] "Then the LORD saw that the wickedness of man *was* great in the earth, and *that* every intent of the thoughts of his heart *was* only evil continually."

LORD *does* not *see* as man sees; for man looks at the outward appearance, but the LORD looks at the heart.'"

Another excellent example would be the prayer that Abraham's slave offered to God prior to meeting Rebekah, Isaac's future wife. Genesis 24:[45] "'But before I had finished **speaking in my heart**, there was Rebekah, coming out with her pitcher on her shoulder; and she went down to the well and drew *water*. And I said to her, 'Please let me drink.'"

The heart and the mind are virtually inseparable. On Sunday mornings and Wednesday nights, church members become witnesses of the confusion when they see preachers and teachers of the WORD point to the muscle in their chests when speaking of the muscle in their minds—homonyms[11].

The Lord did a terrific job of helping believers understand the definition of the word "heart" when referring to the mind. Two of the best scriptures on this subject can be found in Proverbs 23:[7a] "For as he **thinketh** in his **heart**, so is he (KJV)." Proverbs 4:[23] "Keep your heart with all diligence, For out of it *spring* the issues of life." Another great example can be found at Matthew 9:[4] "But Jesus, knowing their thoughts, said, "Why do you **think** evil in your **hearts**?"

---

[11] As a reminder, two words that sound alike and are spelled alike, but have different definitions are called, homonyms.

Clearly, the above verses have nothing to do with the blood pumping muscle in man's chest. Again, both hearts are incredibly essential to sustain life, but in two totally different ways. One keeps the body alive. The other has the ability to help man make worthwhile decisions, wise decisions, righteous decisions, which is why it needs protection, and constant vigilance (Proverbs 4:[23]).

God is a shrouded listener to everything man says verbally and internally. Matthew 12:[36] "But I say to you that for every idle word men may speak, they will give account of it in the day of judgment. [37] For by your words you will be justified, and by your words you will be condemned." Just as man can hear his own thoughts without verbalization, so can God.

For example, when God visited Abraham to tell him about the birth of his son, Sarah, who was in a nearby tent, laughed, but not aloud. Genesis 18:[12] "Therefore Sarah **laughed within** herself, saying, 'After I have grown old, shall I have pleasure, my lord being old also?' [13] And the Lord said to Abraham, 'Why did Sarah laugh, saying, 'Shall I surely bear *a child,* since I am old?' [14] 'Is anything too hard for the Lord? At the appointed time I will return to you, according to the time of life, and Sarah shall have a son.'

¹⁵ But Sarah denied *it,* saying, 'I did not laugh,' for she was afraid. And He said, 'No, but you did laugh!'"

The above verbal exchange is absolutely fascinating. First, God doesn't send Gabriel, the messenger archangel to announce the wonderful news of a promise soon to be fulfilled. He goes to Abraham Himself in the form of 3 men according to verses 1 and 2, signifying that the Father, the Son, and the Holy Spirit were all on the scene.

Second, while God is talking to Abraham, He's keenly aware of every thought on earth. Think of that! Man can be in a restaurant filled to capacity with perhaps 200 different conversations going on all around him, and it sounds like background noise as he can make no sense of what they're saying. But God can hear it all and distinguish who is saying what to whom, not only when they say it, but even before the words leave their mouths.

Third, God is exposing Sarah's lack of faith. And who could blame her when you consider the promise of an heir was made twenty-four years ago when she was sixty-five. Even then it was unbelievable with Abram being seventy-five. Now she's eighty-nine-years-old and Abraham is ninety-nine? Ridiculous! And in Sarah's mind, mere words. As far as she was concerned, it was over. God isn't fair, and he doesn't keep his word to boot! Why would she ever believe now, being past the age of childbearing, no longer having a monthly cycle, and well into menopause?

To her, the greatest flimflam artist of all time had seriously conned them. But then she says, "I didn't laugh." Her thinking was that if it didn't come out of her mouth, she didn't say it. God, on the other hand, is the perpetual listener to the thoughts and intents of the mind. His response reveals the real truth to His people in that He asked a question: "Is anything too hard for the Lord?"

It's clear that each person's thought life is continually monitored by God Himself, which explains why Jesus said, "But I say to you that whoever looks at a woman to lust for her has already committed adultery with her in his heart (Matthew 5:28). Lust is defined as a passionate desire and in this case, the desire is for intimate relations with a woman, single or married. He, therefore, hears people when they say "God is unfair" in their hearts.

Nevertheless, the question remains. Is God unfair? When people pose the question of God's fairness within themselves, they generally mean His fairness to them as opposed to someone else, not across the board. They often compare their sins to the sins of others. People who do this could save themselves lots of anguish if they remembered why they find themselves comparing[12] sins to begin with.

Consider Luke 7:[41] "There was a certain creditor who had two debtors. One owed five hundred denarii, and the other fifty. [42] And when they had nothing with which to repay, he freely forgave them both. Tell Me, therefore, which of them will love him more?" [43] Simon answered and said, "I suppose the *one* whom he forgave more." And He said to him, "You have rightly judged."

People don't fully understand that God is a God of perfection. He will accept nothing less than perfection which is why Christ had to die for the sins of the world. People think that only the worse sinners should be punished, but God knows that even one sin cannot be tolerated in his kingdom. To fully understand why God is a God of perfection, one must understand what happened in The Garden of Eden.

There was only one rule. One law. Genesis 3:[6] "So when the woman saw that the tree *was* good for food, that it *was* pleasant to the eyes, and a tree desirable to make *one* wise, she took of its fruit and ate. She also gave to her husband with her, and he ate." Breaking a single law led to a forfeiture

---

[12] Isaiah 1:[18] "Come now, and let us reason together," Says the Lord, "**Though your sins are like scarlet**, They shall be as white as snow; Though they are red like crimson, They shall be as wool."

of perfection and life itself[13]. But even in a sinful world, he graciously allows man to live and thrive for a time.

Matthew 5:[45b] "for He makes His sun rise on the evil and on the good, and sends rain on the just and on the unjust." I Peter 3:[18a] "For Christ also suffered once for sins, the just for the unjust, that He might bring us to God." Ezekiel 20:[44] "Then you shall know that I *am* the Lord, when I have dealt with you for My name's sake, not according to your wicked ways nor according to your corrupt doings, O house of Israel," says the Lord God."

There are many more scriptures that prove God is not only fair, but He's kind, tolerant, and extremely patient for He gives believers and nonbelievers alike, plenty of time to turn from their evil ways. Deuteronomy 30:[19] "I call heaven and earth as witnesses today against you, *that* I have set before you life and death, blessing and cursing; therefore choose life, that both you and your descendants may live."

If God is unfair, He's unfair in that no matter how many sins a man commits, with the exception of one, he forgives them all. Matthew 12:[31] "Therefore I say to you, every sin and blasphemy will be forgiven men, but the blasphemy *against* the Spirit will not be forgiven men. [32] Anyone who speaks a word against the Son of Man, it will be forgiven him; but

---

[13] Galatians 5:[9] "A little leaven leavens the whole lump".

whoever speaks against the Holy Spirit, it will not be forgiven him, either in this age or in the *age* to come." Every sin would include mass murderers, serial killers, serial rapists, drug cartels, crooked judges, FBI, and police officers who conspire to convict the innocent.

Given the earlier scripture, when true believers are about to enter the pearly gates, what if they are welcomed by the likes of Adolf Hitler, Jack the Ripper, Josef Stalin, Benito Amilcare Andrea Mussolini, or perhaps the notorious cannibal, Jeffrey Lionel Dahmer? Frightening, isn't it? Even more frightening is the image of them remaining in heaven, and the long line of self-righteous men, who never committed one murder, let alone multiple or mass murder, are ushered over to the lake of fire to burn forever.

Matthew 7:[21] "Not everyone who says to Me, 'Lord, Lord,' shall enter the kingdom of heaven, but he who does the will[14] of My Father in heaven. [22] Many will say to Me in that day, 'Lord, Lord, have we not prophesied in Your name, cast out demons in Your name, and done many wonders in Your name?' [23] And then I will declare to them, 'I never knew you; depart from Me, you who practice lawlessness!'

---

[14] II Peter 3:[9] "The Lord is not slack concerning *His* promise, as some count slackness, but is longsuffering toward us, **not willing** that any should perish but that **all** should come to repentance."

Matthew 8:[11] "And I say to you that many will come from east and west, and sit down with Abraham, Isaac, and Jacob in the kingdom of heaven. [12] But the sons of the kingdom will be cast out into outer darkness. There will be weeping and gnashing of teeth."

Self-righteousness is the enemy because it allows the practitioner of it to think, and therefore believe that his "goodness" will be more than enough to make him eligible to enter the pearly gates, but it isn't. The self-righteous are similar to what is *said* about physicians; they make the worse patients. The self-righteous are sick. They're incurably infected with a disease reminiscent of cancer that is both aggressive and malignant.

There is but one destination for the self-righteous if they do not turn to Christ for salvation[15]. Mark 6:[11] "And whoever will not receive you nor hear you, when you depart from there, shake off the dust under your feet as a testimony against them. Assuredly, I say to you, it will be more tolerable for Sodom and Gomorrah in the day of judgment than for that city!"

---

[15] Luke 12: [4] "And I say to you, My friends, do not be afraid of those who kill the body, and after that have no more that they can do. [5] But I will show you whom you should fear: Fear Him who, after He has killed, has power to cast into hell; yes, I say to you, fear Him!"

A Ernest Endeavor

## Chapter 2
## The Original Pimp Part 1

The pimp[16] is a confidence man—better known as a conman who believes wholeheartedly that he can get his victims' attention with words alone, keep them fascinated as they enthusiastically listen without interruption, because they believe every word he utters, as if what he's saying is going to give them the confidence to achieve their dreams—but he's lying even though he acts as if the supposed truth he's telling is of the utmost importance, and needs an immediately audience. But those who believe him, those who trust him, and many women have and do, he will destroy[17] their lives in ways they could never imagine, which is his ultimate goal.

The pimp has a ravenous eye for ingénues of all ages, who don't know the nuances of right and wrong—good and evil. His goal is to incinerate what little truth she has. He does

---

[16] Pimpology is knowing that most, if not all women have a whore inside of them. It is, therefore, the birthright and solemn duty of pimps all over the world, males, and females, to release frustrated females from the torturous state of **virtue** they think they were born in and expose **it** as mythology.

[17] John 10:10 "The thief does not come except to steal, and to kill, and to destroy. I have come that they may have life, and that they may have *it* more abundantly."

this by first telling her what she wants to hear. When her eyes say, "Tell me more," he turns on a spigot of irresistible lies full blast. Before she realizes it, she's his willing slave.

The original pimp was able to turn out Adam's wife with an economy of words—45 to be exact—he was able to convince the woman that God had lied to her; that God couldn't be trusted, and that her husband was a highfalutin *fool* for believing anything God had to say about impending death. With three sentences, the original pimp not only committed a double murder,[18] but became the greatest mass murderer in human history because all men died in Adam.

John 8:[34] Jesus answered them, "Most assuredly, I say to you, whoever commits sin is a **slave of sin**." Romans 6:[6] "knowing this, that our old man was crucified with *Him,* that the body of sin might be done away with, that we should no longer be **slaves of sin**." Romans 6:[16] "Do you not know that to whom you present yourselves **slaves** to obey, you are that one's **slaves** whom you obey, whether of sin *leading* to death, or of obedience *leading* to righteousness?"

Like her husband, the woman was sinless and perfect, too. God doesn't make anything that isn't perfect, which explains the edict given in Matthew 5:[48] "Therefore you shall be perfect,

---

[18] John 8:[44c] "He was a murderer from the beginning, and does not stand in the truth, because there is **no truth in him**."

just as your Father in heaven is perfect." Adam and his wife were not ignorant children who didn't know any better. They were full-grown adults, the equivalent of thirty[19] years[20] of age, much like Christ was when he began his ministry. They had the ability to think and reason as exemplified in The Garden of Eden temptation. A choice was presented[21].

Even the original pimp, Lucifer, was perfect prior to being cast out of heaven.

> Ezekiel 28:[15] "You *were* perfect in your ways from the day you were created, Till iniquity was found in you." Isaiah 14:[12] "How you are fallen from heaven, O Lucifer, son of the morning! *How* you are cut down to the ground, You who weakened the nations! [13] For you have said in your heart: 'I will ascend into heaven, I will exalt my throne above the stars of God; I will also sit on the mount of the congregation On the farthest sides of the north; [14] I will ascend above the heights of the clouds, I will be like the Most High.'"

The man and his wife relinquished all that was good and righteous in them the moment Adam ate fruit from the tree of the knowledge of good and evil. Without perfection, good doesn't exist. In other words, good has a mother and her

---

[19] Genesis 41:[46a] "Joseph was thirty years old when he stood before Pharaoh king of Egypt."

[12] Luke 3:[23a] "Now Jesus Himself began *His ministry at* about thirty years of age."

[21] Deuteronomy 30:19b I have set before you life and death, blessing and cursing; therefore choose life.

name is perfection. Genesis 1:³¹ "Then God saw everything that He had made, and indeed *it was* very good. So the evening and the morning were the sixth day." Matthew 19:¹⁷ "So He [Jesus] said to him, "Why do you call Me good? No one *is* good but One, *that is,* God."

A closer examination of the following scriptures proves that nothing happened when the woman ate the forbidden fruit. But when Adam ate, death entered paradise.

> Genesis 3:⁶ "So when the woman saw that the tree *was* good for food, that it *was* pleasant to the eyes, and a tree desirable to make *one* wise, she took of its fruit and ate. She also gave to her husband with her, and he ate. ⁷ **Then** the eyes of **both** of them were opened, **and they knew** that they *were* naked; and they sewed fig leaves together and made themselves coverings."

When Adam saw his wife eat the forbidden fruit and didn't die, but continued breathing as if nothing happened; as if there was no penalty for disobedience; he monitored the situation, waiting for her to drop dead at the foot of the fruit tree. Adam trusted[22] his eyes and after listening to her persuasively convince[23] him that God was a liar, which is

---

[22] Proverbs 3:⁵ "Trust in the LORD with all your heart, And lean not on your own understanding."
[23] Genesis 3:¹⁷ᵃ Then to Adam He said, "Because you have heeded the voice of your wife."

what her pimp wanted her to do, he, too, ignored God's command not to eat from that tree.

The conversation probably went something like this: "See, Adam. I'm still alive. If God didn't lie to you, why am I still alive? Why should you continue to believe anything God says about anything?" Then she probably took another bite. Then another and another and another. The sound of the apple[24] being bitten crackled in his ears. He probably watched as juice ran down her chin. As she ate, she probably said, "Umm, this is so delicious. This tree has the best fruit than all the trees in the garden."

---

[24] For the record, I know the bible doesn't say the forbidden fruit was an apple. I chose it because of the sound it makes when bitten into, the juice that flows from it when eaten, and the wonderful flavor it offers.

# Chapter 3

# Military Etiquette

Soldiers are expected to follow two kinds of orders. The first kind is a direct order. It's usually verbal and given by someone of higher rank to someone of lower rank. Written instructions are usually called general orders and they are expected to be followed daily. Both can only be countermanded by the person issuing the order or by someone of higher authority. God was and is the highest authority. Therefore, his orders are always to be obeyed. Believers are God's army[25] and it has an organized command structure. The word "command" is a military term that limits the recipient's options. A command isn't a request. It is a direct order.

Genesis 2:[16] And the Lord God commanded **the man**, saying, "Of every tree of the garden you may freely eat; [17] but of the tree of the knowledge of good and evil you shall not eat, for in the day that you eat of it you shall surely die." Notice that God gave no such order to the woman, who at the time

---

[25] Exodus 7:[4] "But Pharaoh will not heed you, so that I may lay My hand on Egypt and bring My **armies** *and* My people, the children of Israel, out of the land of Egypt by great judgments."

the command was issued had not been made. However, it can be reasonably inferred that Adam gave her the order because she told the entity who would prove to be her pimp the following: Genesis 3:2 "And the woman said to the serpent, We may eat the fruit of **the trees** of the garden; 3 but of the fruit of **the tree** which *is* in the midst of the garden, God has said, 'You shall not eat it, nor shall you touch it, lest you die."

God never said, "nor shall you touch it." That was Adam's addendum to God's command. The addendum was within his purview, being king of all the earth. Furthermore, the addendum points to his keen intellect and full understanding of the orders he had "in hand". Moreover, the addendum clarifies what was at stake. Without a doubt Adam knew that violating the order was a death sentence.

For hundreds, perhaps thousands of years, it has been said that prostitution is the oldest profession. It's time for a new paradigm in order to give credit where credit is due. It's time to point the finger of truth at the real culprit; the person who prostituted the first woman in order to destroy her husband who was the image of God at the time of the seduction[26].

---

[26] Genesis 5:3 "And Adam lived one hundred and thirty years, and begot *a son* in his own likeness, after his image, and named him Seth." What was Adam's image after 130 years of sin? Far from what he was—not even close.

Pimping, therefore, should be recognized as the oldest and the most enduring profession. Prostitution is universally defined and known as the exchange of money for coitus. However, prostitution is also defined as the unworthy or corrupt use of one's talents for the sake of personal gain. What did the pre-Christian woman gain? She got an education on what the loss of perfection was like. Satan gained all of humanity as slaves for all time—believers being the *only* exceptions.

Prostitutes rarely gain. They become witting stooges for the personal gain of the man who exclusively controls their minds to their long-term detriment. They lose their youth, their bodies, their minds, and if they don't wake up, they lose their souls.

With the first woman, the definition of long-term is hundreds of years. Her Christian daughters, the ones who have accepted Christ as Lord and Savior, and yet reject God's written orders to follow the dictates of militant feminism and other worldly[27] ways of life, are still being relentlessly pimped for Satan's evil gain.

---

[27] II Corinthians 6:[17] Therefore "Come out from among them And be separate, says the Lord. Do not touch what is unclean, And I will receive you."

When Adam allowed himself to become a "John", he simultaneously sentenced himself to death[28] in an instant. His wife was then retroactively sentenced to death because they were one[29], not two, even though they were also individuals.

The oneness of marriage is one of the most baffling mysteries of all time. How can two different people be one, yet have their own unique identities? Simple. They are created in the image of God. I John 2:[7] "For there are three that bear witness in heaven: the Father, the Word, and the Holy Spirit; and these three are one."

Man is mind, body, and soul; and these three are one. The lack of understanding on the oneness of husband and wife has led to chaos. Just as there is no separation in the oneness of God, there wasn't supposed to be a separation between husband and wife, who represent the oneness of God on earth.

The original pimp declared war on marriage in The Garden of Eden with the intent to separate woman from man with the Independence Initiative, better known as feminism, which over time led to militant feminism.

---

[28] The act of eating the forbidden fruit was the first suicide/murder. Although it isn't often said, suicide is murder.

[29] Genesis 2:[24] "Therefore a man shall leave his father and mother and be joined to his wife, and they shall become one flesh."

*The Elephants In The Room!*

The methods of the Independence Initiative made divorce routine; even in the body of Christ, which should be no surprise since he was able to turn out the perfect woman. Having pimped the only holy woman, is it any wonder that her flawed daughters, the ones who claim to be believers, are equally turned out and consistently war against their husbands, who are believers? The pimp's goal was to turn the believing woman against her God by violating his written orders—to this end, he was very successful.

The rich man and the rich woman define the terms of their future divorce prior to the nuptials. The poor man and the poor woman define the terms of their eventual divorce prior to the marriage ceremony, too, but their divorce doesn't require any legal paperwork. They've already decided what it would take to leave during the betrothal. Marriage, like life, was never supposed to end. Consider Matthew 19:³ The Pharisees also came to Him, testing Him, and saying to Him, "Is it lawful for a man to divorce his wife for *just* any reason?"

⁴ And He answered and said to them, "Have you not read that He who made *them* at the beginning 'made them male and female,' ⁵ and said, 'For this reason a man shall leave his father and mother and be joined to his wife, and the two shall become one flesh'? ⁶ So then, they are no longer two but one

flesh. Therefore what God has joined together, let not man separate."

⁷ They said to Him, "Why then did Moses command to give a certificate of divorce, and to put her away[30]?" ⁸ He said to them, "Moses, because of the hardness of your hearts, permitted you to divorce your wives, but from the beginning it was not so. ⁹ And I say to you, whoever divorces his wife, except for sexual immorality, and marries another, commits adultery; and whoever marries her who is divorced commits adultery."

---

[30] Religious men wanted to divorce their wives. But women could not.

www.ingramcontent.com/pod-product-compliance
Lightning Source LLC
Chambersburg PA
CBHW020015050426
42450CB00005B/480